Between the Wars

Christine Dugan, M.A.Ed.

Publishing Credits

Historical Consultants
Jeff Burke, M.Ed.
Fernando A. Pérez, M.A.Ed.

Editors
Wendy Conklin, M.A.
Torrey Maloof

Editorial Director
Emily R. Smith, M.A.Ed.

Editor-in-Chief
Sharon Coan, M.S.Ed.

Creative Director
Lee Aucoin

Illustration Manager
Timothy J. Bradley

Publisher
Rachelle Cracchiolo, M.S.Ed.

Teacher Created Materials

5301 Oceanus Drive
Huntington Beach, CA 92649-1030
http://www.tcmpub.com
ISBN 978-0-7439-0666-1
© 2008 Teacher Created Materials, Inc.

Table of Contents

Changing Times

Two important world wars were **waged** in the 1900s. The first war lasted from 1914–1918. In the 1920s and 1930s, people called this war the Great War. Many different countries fought in this war. Like in all wars, nations took sides against each other. Today, the Great War is called World War I. In the 1940s, the world waged a second war, World War II. It was even more terrible than the first war. The United States joined in both wars and many American soldiers died.

American soldiers return home from World War I and march in a parade in Minneapolis, Minnesota.

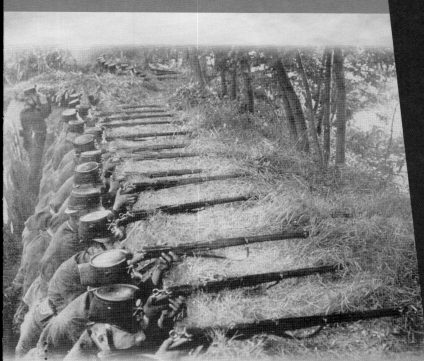

: Soldiers fought from trenches like this during World War I.

Trench Warfare

Soldiers in the world wars fought in trenches. This meant that soldiers on each side dug into the ground. They made underground forts that protected them from enemy fire. Enemy trenches might be as close as 30 yards (27.4 meters) from each other. This made war even more brutal and dangerous.

Saying No

After World War I, countries wanted to unite. They wanted to work together for peace. The League of Nations was formed. America never joined the League of Nations. Many Americans wanted to stay away from the problems in Europe.

These two wars were key events in United States and world history. Many important years passed between the two world wars, and the events of the years between the wars changed the course of United States history.

During those years, the way people lived in the United States changed. For a while, many Americans were successful and wealthy. Then, the Great Depression hit in 1929 and changed everything. Between the wars was a time of great extremes in the United States.

In Style

In the 1920s, style became very important to women. Many young women had short hair, and they wore short dresses. Women started caring more about how they looked and dressed. They read magazines to keep up with the latest fashions.

Flappers

Some women in the 1920s were called **flappers**. They dressed in new fashions. They also acted differently. Flappers were known for dancing, drinking, and smoking in public. Many thought of them as free spirits.

A flapper dances on the cover of *Life* magazine in the 1920s.

Make Us Equal!

During World War I, many women went to work. Men were away fighting in the war. So, women took their jobs in offices and factories. Before this, some people did not think that women were equal to men. These people even felt that women were not smart enough or strong enough to do "men's" work. During the war, women proved those people wrong by succeeding at the same jobs as men.

It might be hard to believe, but women could not vote at the turn of the century. Women **suffragists** (SUHF-rih-jists) had been trying to win the right to vote since the Revolutionary War. Women felt that they should be able to vote just as men could. Not everyone agreed.

This all changed on August 18, 1920. The Nineteenth **Amendment** gave women the right to vote. It was a major victory for women's rights.

After this victory, women looked for other ways to make life equal. Congress finally started to change the laws that allowed unequal practices. At last, people's thoughts about women began to change.

Women picketed in front of the White House in 1917. They wanted to convince President Woodrow Wilson to support women's rights.

Missouri Governor Frederick Gardner signs his state's agreement to ratify the Nineteenth Amendment.

Struggling to Survive

The early 1900s were hard for African Americans. They did not have the same rights as white people. When shopping, African Americans had to enter stores through separate entrances. When thirsty, they could not drink from fountains that said, "Whites Only." This **segregation** (seg-ruh-GAY-shuhn) based on their skin color was unfair. African Americans fought hard for their country in World War I, and yet they were still treated badly at home.

W. E. B. DuBois was an important leader in the early years of the NAACP. This is the NAACP office where DuBois worked.

Langston Hughes wrote poems, novels, short stories, newspaper columns, and plays.

In 1909, a special group was formed. This group believed in standing up for the rights of African Americans. They called themselves the National Association for the Advancement of Colored People (NAACP). The group thought people needed to know that segregation was wrong. The NAACP is still active today.

At this time, it was important for African Americans to speak up. African American authors began writing about segregation. W. E. B. DuBois and Langston Hughes were two of these important authors.

Different Kinds of Relief

The government often treated African Americans unequal. During the Great Depression, people received government aid. It was money to help them live. African Americans, however, received smaller amounts of money than white people.

Life as a Sharecropper

Many African Americans worked as sharecroppers. That means they raised crops on land that belonged to someone else. Sharecroppers had to share some of their crops with the landowners. Landowners often cheated the sharecroppers. It was a very difficult life for the African Americans. There is a good book about this time period. It is called *Roll of Thunder, Hear My Cry* by Mildred D. Taylor. It tells about a family of African American sharecroppers.

Singing Outside

Marian Anderson was a famous African American singer in the 1930s. In 1939, she wanted to sing in Washington, D.C. The city was still segregated. So, she was not allowed to sing in Constitutional Hall because she was African American. First Lady Eleanor Roosevelt and others were furious. Instead, she was invited to sing at the Lincoln Memorial. She sang for 75,000 people outside. A few weeks later, she sang at the White House.

From the South to the North

Louis Armstrong got his start in New Orleans. Then he moved north to New York. He started making music with Bessie Smith and others. People from all over the world became fans.

A Renaissance in Harlem

In the 1920s, a **migration** (my-GRAY-shuhn) took place. Many African Americans moved from the South to the North and West. They hoped to escape segregation. They settled in busy cities, like New York City, and looked for jobs.

One part of New York City is known as Harlem. An amazing **renaissance** (reh-nuh-SAWNTS) occurred there. A renaissance is a time of great change and growth. African American writers, singers, and poets thrived as they wrote and sang about their lives. Their words touched the lives of other African Americans. This time was known as the Harlem Renaissance.

Many of these artists are still famous. Louis Armstrong was known for his amazing trumpet playing. Bessie Smith was a famous singer. Duke Ellington was a well-known jazz musician. Zora Neale Hurston wrote incredible African American literature. Some historians call this the start of the Civil Rights Movement.

Many famous performers played at the Cotton Club in Harlem.

Bessie Smith signed a record deal with Columbia Records® in 1923. Her first record sold over 750,000 copies.

Literature of the Day

Many new authors and poets **published** books in the 1920s. Some readers today think these books are among the best from the twentieth century. Many books from this decade are still very popular today.

T. S. Eliot was a famous poet from this time. He wrote a book of poems called *The Waste Land* that is among the most important poetry written in the twentieth century. Eliot's poems explain how America was changing during the early decades.

F. Scott Fitzgerald is another famous author from the 1920s. His books often described people who were rich and how they lived life to the fullest. *The Great Gatsby*, a brilliant novel by Fitzgerald, was published in 1925.

F. Scott Fitzgerald and his most-famous novel

Virginia Woolf was a great writer of this time.

A Famous Cousin

F. Scott Fitzgerald was named after his distant cousin. His cousin's name was Francis Scott Key. Key was the **composer** (kuhm-POH-zuhr) of the national anthem of the United States.

Gertrude Stein

Gertrude Stein was known for her repetition (rep-uh-TISH-uhn) in writing. One famous line she wrote is "A rose is a rose is a rose is a rose."

Men were not the only writers back then, of course. Many women were also writing great works. Virginia Woolf was one of these female writers. Woolf believed in equal rights for women. Her books reflected those ideas. One of her most famous books, *A Room of One's Own,* was published in 1929.

Another female author was Gertrude Stein. Authors, painters, and other artists respected her views. They came to her for advice and wisdom.

Painting of Gertrude Stein by Pablo Picasso

What a Deal!

The first Model T car cost $825. By 1912, the cars cost $575. By the 1920s, the Model Ts cost just $290. This was because the assembly line allowed Ford to make many cars at one time. So, each car was less expensive to create.

Only Black Cars

At first, Model T cars came in one color—black. People believe that Henry Ford once claimed, "You can paint it any color, so long as it is black." After 1925, other colors slowly became available.

Riding with Style

Imagine your life without a car to take you places. Henry Ford was the **industrialist** who made cars so popular. He made the first **reliable** (rih-LIE-uh-buhl) car, the Model T, in 1908.

At first, it took a long time for workers to build a car. Someone had to place all the pieces by hand. Then, Ford invented the **assembly line**. Each person on an assembly line installed one part of the car as it moved along a **conveyor belt**. In that way, each car got all the parts it needed. This meant that workers could make many cars each day.

The assembly line kept getting faster. In 1912, it took 12.5 hours to make one car. By 1925, it took only 1.5 hours. Less production time meant lower costs. In no time, cars were everywhere.

By the 1920s, cars were very popular in the United States. Businesses started needing drivers. Garages and gas stations spread across towns, and the country needed better roads, too. Automobiles changed America.

These Model Ts are coming off the Ford assembly line. They all looked the same.

Henry Ford was a great leader in the automobile industry.

A Dark Day in History

Many things changed during the first two decades of the 1900s. Women became more active outside the home. African Americans expressed themselves in the arts. Authors wrote about life during the time period. Many people owned cars and felt successful. The mood in the United States was happy and carefree.

The mood of the country quickly changed on October 29, 1929. Until then, people had bought **stocks** with borrowed money. People all over the country felt rich. On that day, the stock market crashed. All of a sudden, people owed money to the banks because they had to pay back what they had borrowed. Unfortunately, people did not have the money. Many businesses closed, and people lost their jobs and homes.

Men and women without jobs wait in long lines to get soup and bread during the Great Depression.

: Tiny shacks make up this Hooverville outside of New York City.
: People who had lost their homes lived here.

Where Is Hooverville?

When some people had to give up their homes, they lived in run-down shacks. Many shacks would be set up in small areas. These areas became known as Hoovervilles. They were named after President Herbert Hoover. People felt that the president was doing little to end the depression. They blamed him for their troubles.

Black Tuesday

The day the stock market crashed is known as Black Tuesday. This was because the day was so sad and awful for America. This day was the start of the Great Depression.

Without jobs, there was no money to buy food. To survive, families had to sell their possessions. Many people became **desperate** (DES-puh-ruht) for help.

Some people decided to look for jobs in new towns. They packed up their few belongings and left their homes. Many of them could not afford new homes, so whole families lived out of their cars. If a family did not have a car, the entire family had to walk from town to town.

The Great Depression took place during the years that followed the stock market crash. Surviving these difficult years was very hard for most Americans. It took the country many years to recover, and it was a sad, hard time in American history.

Dust Clouds

Weather was extreme in the Midwest at this time. Rain was scarce. So there were major dust storms that lasted hours or days. There would be so much dust in the air you could not see in front of you. This made life even harder for farmers.

A Picture of the Times

Many photographs tell the story of the depression. Dorothea Lange was a photographer at the time. She took pictures of everyday people trying to survive. Her work tells the story of the hardships of the Great Depression.

This picture of a migrant mother may be Lange's most famous photograph.

On the Road Again

This sudden change in life forced many people to move. As the 1930s began, families started moving from their homes to new towns or states. These people were called **migrants** (MY-gruntz). They were looking for fresh starts. Many people headed west because they thought life would be better in California.

Some of the newcomers to California were not welcomed there. Californians nicknamed them the Okies, which referred to that fact that some of them came from Oklahoma. Californians thought that the Okies were poor and dirty. The people in California did not want the Okies to move there.

The migrants in California lived in camps. The camps were not very nice places to live, but at least they had tents for sleeping, something to eat, and places to shower. In the camps, families made friends and helped each other. Many migrants found work on farms by moving from camp to camp. Life was still very difficult, but things were starting to look more positive for some Americans.

Droughts caused dust storms like this one in Kansas.

This migrant family lives in a car. They are on their way to California for a better life.

A Little Fun Now and Then

During the Great Depression, people looked for things to take their minds off their troubles. They longed to think about something other than their own difficulties. In the early 1920s, movies cost between a nickel and a dime. About half of all Americans went to the movies each week. At first, all movies were silent. With no sound, the actors had to tell stories without talking. Then, in the late 1920s, movies began to have sound. People were excited to see these new films, called "talkies."

Clara Bow was a well-known actress during this time. She began her acting career by winning a contest in a magazine. The prize was a role in a film.

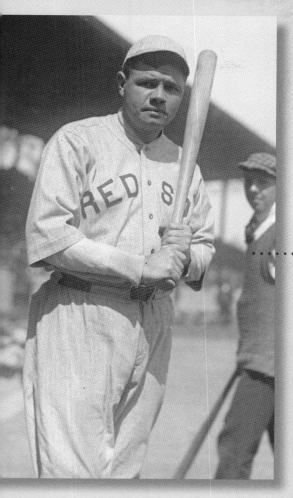

Babe Ruth began his baseball career with the Boston Red Sox. In 1920, he moved to the New York Yankees. Some people believed that this move placed a curse on the Red Sox.

The House That Ruth Built

Yankee Stadium is a famous ballpark. It opened in New York in 1923. In the first game played there, Babe Ruth hit the park's first home run. Yankee Stadium was nicknamed "The House that Ruth Built."

The "It" Girl

Clara Bow was a famous actress in the 1920s. She starred in many silent films. One film, called *It*, helped her get the nickname of "The 'It' Girl." This term is still used to describe popular entertainers today.

Another favorite pastime was baseball. Baseball games were fun for people of all ages. The game had been around for many years. In 1935, the first night games took place. The New York Yankees were a successful team then. Babe Ruth played for the Yankees. Many baseball fans think he was one of the best players ever. The sport helped people forget their own hardships.

Hold Your Sign

Workers on strike hold picket signs. These signs have messages for the people in charge. A picket sign might say, "Better Working Conditions in Our Factory!" Or, signs might ask for more money. Unions often wanted better working hours, too.

Sitting Down on the Job

Most striking workers walked around holding picket signs. But one famous strike was a sit-down strike. At a car factory in 1936, workers sat down while working. The strike lasted for 44 days.

These two union women are on strike in New York City.

On Strike!

The Great Depression brought hard times to Americans. People realized that they needed to work hard to make life better. This made them think about how workers were treated, and many people felt that workers needed better options.

Workers formed groups called **labor unions**. The unions protected workers from unfair treatment. Joining together gave the workers more power. If one worker asked for better pay, the boss might fire him. If 500 workers asked, the boss had to listen. Otherwise, the workers could strike, and that would leave the company with no workers. Without workers, the factory would shut down, and then the business would not make any money.

Of course, not many bosses liked the unions. Often, arguments turned violent. Sometimes other people had to step in and help solve problems. Unions still play an important role in American businesses today.

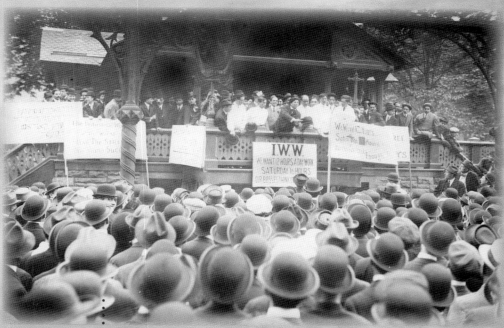

The Barber's Union held a strike in Union Square, New York.

President Franklin Roosevelt described how he planned to get America back on its feet.

First Lady Eleanor Roosevelt meets with a group of women and listens carefully to what they have to say. She then shares their concerns with the president.

A New and Promising Leader

In 1933, Americans elected Franklin Delano Roosevelt to be president. Roosevelt got to work right away. President Roosevelt made a famous **inaugural** (ih-NAW-gyuh-ruhl) speech. He said, "The only thing we have to fear is fear itself." His brave words during the Great Depression made people trust him. They believed he would get the country back on track.

Roosevelt had a plan called the New Deal. In this plan, he signed many new bills designed to help those in need. His new programs gave much-needed jobs to the unemployed. Instead of living in tents or on the streets, he wanted them to have homes. Instead of making young children work, he wanted them back in schools. This plan was successful and seemed to lift the American spirit.

The First Lady, Eleanor Roosevelt, was a big help as well. She traveled around the country. She wanted to get to know the American people. She heard their concerns, and then told her husband about them. Without her, President Roosevelt would not have understood Americans so well.

FDR's Health

President Roosevelt suffered from **polio** (POH-lee-oh). He used a wheelchair or a cane to get around. Polio made it hard for Roosevelt to travel. His wife, Eleanor Roosevelt, often traveled in his place.

Alphabet Soup

People called Roosevelt by his initials—FDR. Many of his new programs were also referred to by initials. The National Recovery Act, for example, was called the NRA. The Civilian Conservation Corps was the CCC. And, the Works Progress Administration was the WPA. This made some people call Roosevelt's work the "alphabet soup programs." These programs helped bring jobs to thousands of Americans while rebuilding America.

Changes Around the World

In the late 1930s, things were changing around the world. War had broken out in Europe again. There were conflicts in Asia, as well. The United States knew it could not live in **isolation** (i-suh-LAY-shuhn), but the country was not ready to join the war. So, the United States decided to lend a hand.

Lend-Lease Program

The United States started to sell, lend, and give items to the countries fighting against Germany, Italy, and Japan in World War II. Congress gave FDR the power to decide how much help to lend other countries. Great Britain, China, and the USSR received most of the lend-lease aid.

Fireside Chats

Roosevelt began a radio show where he talked to the people each week. These were called Fireside Chats. People sat in their homes and listened to him talk to them. They began to feel like he understood their hardships. To this day, presidents have continued using the radio and television to speak to the people. History has taught presidents that it is important to talk to American citizens.

President Roosevelt started the Lend-Lease Program. He saw this as a way to help his own country, too. In no time, factories were busy making products for the war. Countries overseas needed products such as blankets, uniforms, ships, and airplanes. This kind of work required a lot of workers, and there were more jobs being created every day.

With all these new jobs, more women were starting to work, too. And, African Americans were working at new jobs. **Wages** were getting higher for workers. This helped people who had struggled for so long during the depression.

Making materials for World War II helped to end the Great Depression. America was finally getting back on its feet.

Franklin Roosevelt gave many Fireside Chats during his years as president.

The United States started the Lend-Lease Program to aid the war effort without joining the war. This map shows the aid routes.

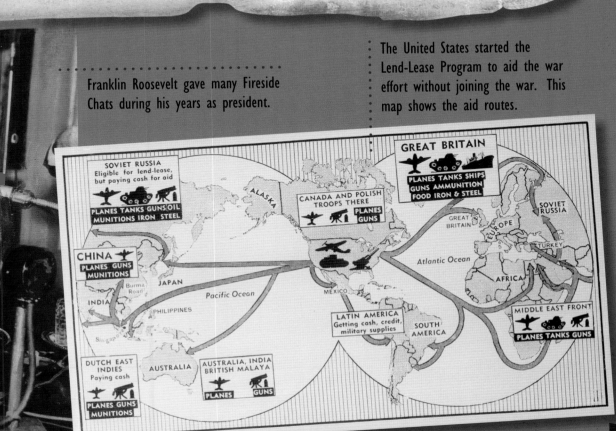

Back to War

President Roosevelt closely watched the world events from 1939 to 1941. Some countries wanted the United States to join the war. However, Americans were still not sure.

This changed on December 7, 1941. On that day, Japan attacked the United States. The Japanese bombed a military base in Hawaii called Pearl Harbor. More than 2,400 Americans were killed. The United States Congress declared war on Japan.

People in Pearl Harbor were surprised by the Japanese attack.

Adolf Hitler was the ruler of Nazi Germany.

A Four-Time President

President Roosevelt was elected four times. This is more than any other president in history. In fact, the Twenty-Second Amendment to the Constitution states that presidents can only be elected twice. Roosevelt died on April 25, 1945. Vice President Harry S. Truman took over the White House. President Truman helped end World War II.

Two Surrenders

The fighting in Europe ended on May 8, 1945. Germany surrendered. Four months later, Japan surrendered. The fighting in Japan ended on September 2, 1945.

Germany and Japan were part of the **Axis powers**. So, Germany declared war on the United States. The United States had to fight back. That meant the United States had to fight on two sides of the world at the same time. One enemy was in Asia and the other was in Europe.

At this point, life in the United States had changed. Instead of worrying about food and jobs, Americans focused on surviving World War II. They worked at home and overseas to support the war effort. The end of the Great Depression was finally here because of the war.

Glossary

amendment—a change made to the Constitution; two-thirds of the states must agree to the change

assembly line—an arrangement of workers where an item moves along a conveyer belt and workers add to the item as it moves along until the whole piece is assembled

Axis powers—Germany, Japan, and Italy in World War II

composer—someone who writes songs

conveyor belt—a continuously moving band that transports things from one point to another

desperate—to worry or be in need

flappers—young woman in America in the 1920s with a certain style and attitude

inaugural—relating to when a president takes office

industrialists—a person who owns or controls a manufacturing business

isolation—to be alone and not worry about other countries' problems

labor unions—a group of workers formed to protect their rights

Midwest—states in the middle of the United States

migrants—people who have moved from one region to another

migration—to move from one place to another

polio—a virus that affects nerve cells in the spinal cord and may cause paralysis

published—to have printed for the public

reliable—dependable

renaissance—a time of growth and change

segregation—forced separation of groups based on race

stocks—shares in a company that show ownership and a right to receive part of the profits

suffragists—those who support extending the right to vote to others, especially women

waged—to carry on or fight

wages—the money received for doing a job

Index

Image Credits